What Remains

Books by Jim Doss

Learning to Talk Again
The Last Gold of Expired Stars,
translations of Georg Trakl

What Remains

Jim Doss

LOCH RAVEN PRESS   SYKESVILLE, MD   2017

The majority of these poems were written between 2005 and 2015 and many of them have appeared in various poetry journals on the internet

Cover drawing: *Weary* by Kenny A. Chaffin. More of Kenny's work can be seen at https://kennyc.deviantart.com/.

Library of Congress Control Number: 2017914135

ISBN 13: 978-0982185469

Loch Raven Press
140 Milrey Drive, Suite L
Sykesville, MD 21784
www.lochravenpress.com

Contents

What Remains

Lynchburg

Years ago I read the headlines from up north—
Hustler magazines still in their brown wrappers
piled high in gasoline flames, the store shelves cleared
as if by a plague of locust; Jerry Falwell and The Moral Majority
versus Larry Flint in the courts and minds of America.

Returning today, I drive by teenagers who browse stores
on Main Street. The studs in their pierced bellybuttons and lips
gleam in the sun. Tattoos decorate their bodies, not with pictures
from the Sistine Chapel, but snakes, barbed wire, spiders.

I head into the openness of church steeples rising above
a canopy of green—one on every corner. Radio preachers
clog the dial with blue grass, gospel and new age Jesus.
Mansions built from slaves, tobacco, coal, and railroads,
now apartment buildings, grey beneath scabby
coats of paint—the old money long since fled. I pass

the African Room with its cardboard *No Whites Allowed* sign
in the window, the abandoned shoe factory where my grandfather
worked slowly collapsing into a backwater of weeds and rats,
and the little league baseball fields at Miller Park where dreams
always fall just outside the foul lines. I turn into Fairview
Heights, past where the Falwell brothers raised Cain
before they had their vision of God on the road to Damascus.

I park my car in a field my father set on fire when he was a boy
playing with matches, then hid trembling in the underbrush
as the fire engines arrived. The sirens that hurt my ears
now are not for his deeds, but some other world
I know nothing about.
                    The town that lives inside me
extends its arms in acceptance of all that I am and am not.

Point of Honor

Lynchburg

Dueling pistols no longer flash
in the sunlight. What stray bullets
fly here have nothing to do
with love or honor. Territory
is everything. The dandified gentlemen
who faced each other in the morning sun
have long disappeared into the mist
that rises from the James no different
than it did two hundred years ago.
Chrome handlebars slide
through afternoon into the night
peddled by boys with cell phones
and dreadlocks that snap
like whips in the wind.
Something exchanges hands
beneath the shadow of statues,
on street corners, through car windows.
In a private room
Caesar and Pompey drink
to their new partnership
watched over by the uneasy eyes
of minions—their destinies
of blood linked together
by the black-handled revolvers
tucked into their belts.

At Edankraal

the home of Anne Spencer

Whoever comes here could spend
a lifetime in this garden in a single afternoon,
his lips fluttering
like a butterfly from one rose to another,
reciting words he's never used before,
his fingers tracing the subtle hieroglyphics of a dogwood leaf
as he learns to speak this new language,
stroking the serrated edge of a mint leaf
without getting cut,
fondling the blooms and tendrils of the morning glory
as it plays the trellis like a harp.
He could walk trails lined by boxwoods
where phantom deer turn into girls chased by satyrs
as the evening mist descends;
or drop rocks into the lily pond
where the statue of a Nubian boy,
bared to the shoulders, rises like Adam
from creation's mud. He could imagine the breath he feels stirring
on his cheek is God
still walking through the groves, sighing with satisfaction.
And when it's time to leave
he'll slip the seeds he's borrowed into his pocket,
brush back the few remaining strands of hair left on his head,
walk nonchalantly toward his car
to take them home, watch them germinate as he grows older,
realizing he knows nothing,
nothing at all
about this world that is constantly beginning.

Grandmother in Heaven

Darkness eases between the leaves
of the maple as you walk with a basket
of windfall gathered from Seelman's orchard.

In it you've gathered red and gold apples,
green pears with a touch of blush on their cheeks,
and blackberries oozing with juice. You follow

a dirt path raked clean by chicken claws
to the covered porch with its glider,
rocking chairs, and moths circling globes of light.

You hesitate by a long-forgotten door
where grey wood reveals the soul hidden
beneath a skin of flaking paint.

It's years before your second son
will lay in an improvised incubator
made out of blankets, a basting pan

and the oven's low heat as you nurse
his fight for life with a medicine dropper
filled with your own breast milk.

It's decades before the last heart attack
will turn your red hair silky white
as the hydrangeas blooming in your yard.

Now you step across the threshold
to become your father's plain Irish daughter again,
greeted by the silence of his pipe smoke.

It follows you into the kitchen, watches
you empty the basket onto the oak table,
count the pieces one by one

while he sleeps in a lounge chair,
newspaper folded into wings
across the rising and falling of his chest.

Tonight you will sit in your room,
braid a love knot before the mirror,
waiting for the black haired German boy,

face sunburned from the fields, but cleanly washed,
to toss a pebble against your window,
show you there is nothing plain about the darkness.

What the Ancestors Left

Where the wills were written and signed
in black ink and the executors carried out the wishes
of the dead a summer boathouse now stands.

Its white clapboard shimmers in the noon heat
no more than a stone's throw from the hum of power turbines
that generate enough electricity to light the city we live in,

and the spillway that greens and darkens with age
in the trickle of runoff. I rent a canoe, push out
into the reservoir's blue waters to glide

like a bird across the reflection of sky and clouds.
I hug the eastern shoreline where my Great Uncles steered
their locomotives across the railroad tracks that ran beside

the Blackwater and the channel it cut through the hills.
Looking down I can see the grey ribbon of gravel,
the trellis still supporting its steel ready for another cargo run.

My shadow moves like smoke to the next cove,
Bill Zimmerman's old pasture. The fence that couldn't hold
his wild stallion when the wind blew in the right direction

steps from water now to pace a shoreline it can't escape.
Further down, the path from the gate to the house
is hidden by a snarl of dark tree limbs and boards

bulldozed into a scorched pile of rubbish
bass and catfish grow fat around not thinking
of the fingers that left their prints on the doorknobs,

hung clothes on the line, watched the waters take
what they'd worked generations to accumulate.
I can go back eighty years, imagine my grandfather

shaking hands with old man Z on the front porch,
their gentleman's agreement to buy the bottomland
that sometimes flooded, but was as dark as his hair,

and produced a good crop four years out of five.
What is a treasure to some means little to others.
I paddle through history like a man lost in a recurring dream.

The blister that darkens and grows on my palm is my mark,
the sign of my native land, a hillside that rises above these waters
to keep everything I want to save from dissolving.

Poem Spoken in My Mother's Voice

It wasn't a rumor. Daddy
was dying from Brights. All day long,
he lay on that old feather bed,
swollen, heart pounding
like a bird that wanted to fly
out of his chest. Roosevelt
spoke to us on the radio
about the Government and jobs,
drought, the cattlemen and farmers
who weren't cooperating
with The New Deal. Our fields
were plowed, and waited
to be parted like the Red Sea,
but the miracle never occurred.
The soil baked into hard clay.
The gravedigger could barely
open his door into the ground.
I heard my aunts and uncles
whisper over the casket
times were hard, too hard
for charity. The younger kids
played tag around the mound
of freshly dug earth, while mother,
barely into her twenties and pregnant
again, was carried to the car.
For weeks I kept that terrible secret inside me,
where I longed to watch it grow
into fields of corn and beans,
stalls of fattened cows and pigs,
berries that ripened into jewels around
the fenceline while my father's footsteps
followed me everywhere I went.
But when the car came
to take us to the orphanage
mother barely wept,
waved to us from the front door
dressed in her Sunday best,
a silent figure receding into the dust
as her kids' dirty hands now clung to my skirt.

Goose Creek

I dreamed I married
and lived in Goose Creek
in a set of rooms above
the general store
where I swept floors, stacked cans,
sold printed fabric by the yard,
dried beans by the pound.

My wife was tall and blonde,
severe in her Christian ways.
Her hair smelled always
like wet ashes; her eyes
glowed into torches at dusk,
and our children walked
to a one-room schoolhouse
over muddy roads.

Men from the east passed through
longing for gold, timber,
whiskey and easy women;
men from the west,
broken, penniless,
often sick, retreated
toward the mercy
of homes they hoped
would take them back.

By oil lamp
I wrote my journal of dust
in railroad whistles,
unsmelted nuggets,
and bloodied knuckles.
Each year was a stack
of spring cordwood
that weathered into winter fire.

But that last season
the wind knocked
at my door and no one answered.
It prowled alleyways,
polished the graveyard stones
and fences grey with age

as the coyotes, inching
ever closer into town,
sang their hymns
from moon-bright hillsides.

My family headed south
on a train flanked by migrating starlings.
I stood alone on Main Street
surrounded by houses
dark and still, the jail chained shut,
church door off its hinges.
I searched for a light in any broken window,
a footstep in the gravel,
a voice to scrape away the silence.

With a jagged
piece of glass I carved a map
of my heart in the frozen dirt,
unbuttoned my coat, let my clothes
fall to the ground.
                      Soon
the wind leafed through
the history of my ribs,
memorized the journal of gnawed words
I'd so carefully tended
for over thirty years
to pass my story on
to whoever comes next.

She Had One of Them

beautiful faces and blonde hair
like those famous nobodies
splashed all over the TV screens

her mother was still shapely
and drove a red convertible
step-daddy one and two were blueblooded drunks
with number three already on the way

the grandmother couldn't hear
a word that was spoken
wore a star sapphire blue as the coldest pump handle
she told of bygone days
when the house was painted oyster shell white
and the colored folk still worked the fields

back then she drove a Lincoln
to meet the trains coming into town
loaded with coal solid oak furniture
romance novels from New York perfumes from Paris
and those old-money no-counts from New Orleans
with dice tucked in the band of their fedoras
plump from squandering the family fortune

how many do the stories say she married
the legend grows like kudzu
or blood violets
or fingers pounding a boogie woogie piano
at the local speakeasies

the granddaughter was just like her
smelling of honeysuckle that grows by the sea
playfully cruel like a wasp
dancing on the lip of a soda bottle

I could say it's hell growing up
around here where ladies are judged
by the number of men
their love has put in the ground
without even having a kiss
or a longing glance thrown my way

but I have all these weeds to pull

weeds blooming in the family plot
casting their seed everywhere
my silver dollars can't reach

Allegory of Love in a Time of Drought

Before we met
I was a weed in your dreams,
my hair already gone to seed.

Thousands of brown
whirligigs helicoptered
through the air
to twist a taproot
into your moonlight garden.

One took hold there,
a perfect clone:
green, tall, with wild
hair that rubbed
against the clapboard
like a musician
in a hillbilly band.

It's music played all night,
then vanished
as daylight's glint
reflected off your red shears

onto my image
walking up the road
to ask for
a drink of well-water.

Orphan

The hand that took mine
was not called love, or caring, or tenderness.
It was calloused and hard
like the boots they put on my feet,
the comb they raked through my hair.

Lye soap could not scrub its touch off of me,
a stain that barely faded with time,
a birthmark that blended in with the burn
of sun-scorched fields where hay
and corn were bundled for the livestock.

Parents, what are they but memory
in this place where only the present counts,
where chores always lie in front,
and the Gothic spires of buildings shadow
the dormitories filled with rows of beds.

Childhood of dirt and beans,
ivy covering the railings, the eyes
of all who would peer inside
see there is nothing here,
nothing but the longing to be held.

Ancestry

I grew tired of being a man.
So I stripped down and fell asleep
beside a stream, let God
have His way with me. Soon
I dreamed I was a woman hoeing
tobacco fields in blistering heat.
Dragonflies flew from my mouth
when I tried to speak. My hands bled
into overripe raspberries still gripping
a withered vine. The föhn
kept lifting my dress, bending
the leaves into mocking faces.
I longed for a drink of well-water
sweetened with molasses to wash
the taste of dust from my tongue.
I was growing faint enough to see
Ezekiel's wheel. Then I heard a galloping
come from the north, something lifted
me off of my feet. My thighs clutched
the neck of a horse, the rub of coarse,
matted mane. I gulped hot darning needles
of air. We stopped at a house where pigs
wallowed under the floorboards and fear
crept through my insides like moonshine
through a still. I wanted to say
place your head on the brown soil
of my belly, listen to the children grow.
But by then my voice was nothing but wings.

Conception

At one time I was nothing more than a random thought swirling around Riverside Park looking for a home. The wind carried me where it wanted. I blew past the statue of a Confederate general whose face pointed to the stars. I drifted over the decayed packet boat Marshall that carried Stonewall Jackson's body up the James to Lexington, swirled past a black Buick with steamy windows parked by the woods rocking to a doo-wop beat.

I hitched a ride on the back of a firefly, followed a creek into a stand of locust where a dirt path led to a cul-de-sac. Brick houses lined both sides of the street. Cones of light fell from the streetlamps where two men swung imaginary 4 irons over cans of beer and watched their balls land next to the pin on the 18th green at Augusta. Their wives laughed from the kitchen window nursing martinis as a pot roast simmered in the oven. Diced carrots, onions and potatoes awaited their moment of glory lined up on a serving plate with a turkey painted in the middle.

I floated over the roofs of several houses before sifting through a screen into an open window. A man rose from the couch to switch off *77 Sunset Strip*, then walked over to the hi-fi, stacked songs on the spindle by Nat King Cole, Perry Como, and Andy Williams. As the needle's arm lifted and set down his hand reached out. A woman's hand folded into his. He drew her close, settled her head against his shoulder. They swayed in the soft breeze of music like a wind chime creating their own harmonies. Her hands stroked the small of his back. His arms encircled her as if he could erase all memories of the orphanage with his promise of a lifetime of growing old together. They danced for what seemed like hours with their eyes closed to the world as headlights swept by their windows. No meanness, no harsh words, no switches striking the back of the legs or arms. Only tenderness like she'd never known, and I came into being, a single cell, hardly random at all, already growing by powers of two.

Father, Husband

Boy

He looks so unreal lying there,
a wax figure resting on white pillows.
When I touch his face, it isn't flesh I feel,
but the coolness of stones polished in mountain streams.
When I look at his lips, they are silent doorways
that will never open again to tell a joke,
or echo with laughter. When I imagine his eyes,
they are death swans gliding over the dark lakes of memory
where the film clips of life are replayed over and over.
Who knew his heart was a tree made of glass
where each leaf glowed with its own wound,
where each wound merged into the other
until they burned up inside of him?
Time has already begun to swallow his footprints,
dissolve everything he's ever touched into dust.
Soon he will be no more than an echo in my dreams, that faint map
painted behind my eyelids darkening half of the world.

Girl

He will not stay buried,
the part of him that is a reflection of me,
that maze of mirrors hanging
over my bed like a network of gleaming spiderwebs.
There is no escaping the emptiness
reflected there, no matter
how many paper coffins I bridge together
to reach the other side. Like a blind person, I dream
of total darkness, distant voices echoing
his departure, not even Helen Keller's pearl
glowing visibly in my palm, that white seed of truth
that is the most beautiful thing in her life.
I dream of quarries where great slabs of granite
are hauled out of the earth
and carved into wings of flame. I dream of a hand
reaching out of the mirror to pull me into the fading twilight,
the nest of bones I must leave behind for another child

to sleep in and dream of this day.

Mother, Wife

Will it be this way eight,
ten, fifteen years from now?
This emptiness like the earth
has given way beneath my feet,
like the grave has been dug for me too,
yet I'm to keep on waking, eating, breathing
as though nothing happened,
as though my numbness will blossom
into a thistle that I can touch each night
to know I am still alive. When I shut my eyes
I still see him in his Marine dress blues
or on the white sands of Miami Beach
slipping further and further away from me,
feel his touch growing faint like the brush of wings.
I am lost, forgotten, left at the door of the orphanage again
with two children in tow, two mouths calling out
for me to be both mother and father,
when I have nothing to offer but the ashes of my grief.

The Unvanquished

They had that "you can trust me with your life" smile,
the twinkle of a shooting star in their eye,
and the swoop of hair cresting the forehead.
How long had I watched my father and the President
crack jokes in stereo, one on TV, the other in the living room.
Now there was no joy seeing the caissons roll
past the Capital, the riderless horse with boots turned
backward in the stirrups clop its lonely path toward forever.
Why must people die? I asked the blank stare,
the upturned cuffs, the pencil holder
in the shirt pocket, the pipe with its smell of gunpowder,
my words reverberating in the silence
of the grassy knoll. Three years later his own heart
assassinated itself, a single bullet coursing
through his veins, the ex-Marine felled
by what he couldn't see coming,
the triangle of flag presented to me by the honor guard,
the snap salute of a grateful country,
that question still burning in my mind like an eternal flame.

My Father's Left Hand

turned the yellow-handled screwdriver
to bind copper wire and receptacle together
so electricity could resume flowing like blood.

It gripped the pencil that scrawled these equations
in a black field book, longitude and latitude,
those spots where the plumb bob fell to earth,

and it pushed his black glasses up on the bridge
of his nose as he smiled at the lumberyard salesman
loading southern pine 2x4s in the bed of a pickup.

I can see the outline of that hand now in mine,
the nails pink and ridged, the fingers long as stems
rising from thawing ground, how it gripped the seams

of a baseball showing a young boy how to throw
a heater right down the heart of the plate,
or pushed golf ball and tee into manicured grass.

And these lives my own hand guides, will they ask
the length of my lifeline, am I now at the zenith of my powers,
or do they just want to be comforted by my touch?

My dad's left hand wore the gold ring that bound him to us,
this symbol of trust, now dimming in the half-light of memory,
where wildflowers climb a stone of chiseled letters.

Primitive Medicine

The middle finger on his left hand was lopped off
at the first joint, not through some accident
at the shoe factory, but from a blood clot
that turned the finger into a swollen purple sapling
that the country doctor removed with a cleaver.
He would rub it as he talked, a kind of nervous habit,
like the bitter-sweet reminder of the son that was now missing
from his life. His education stopped in the third grade
where mine continued, but he would spend hours
walking me through his hardpan life as we shoveled
black, dusty chunks of coal into the glowing belly of the furnace,
or walked his buzzing hillside garden hoeing weeds
around his precious strawberries and tomatoes. Sometimes
we'd just soak in the gold of the sun, pop his Chevy Belair hood,
go through the engine parts while he'd make some minor repair
or adjustment as the smoke of his filterless Pall-Mall
clouded my brain with dreams of nicotine. By day
he was a teetotaling, church-going man with a love
of country and wife. Some nights he was rumored
to hit the white lightning with his buddies, get overly friendly
with other women. I never saw this side of him,
just the old field hand who had no time for tomfoolery
like throwing a baseball or football, who like a plow horse
never stopped working, never stopped turning the soil,
driving a nail into planks of wood, or gripping a paint brush
to slap a coat of new on what was earned with his sweat alone.
Yet he always had time to help a neighbor, or sit and visit
with a lonely soul. It was here in this little house
on an oversized lot in the not so good part of town
that I learned what it meant to be a grandfather
to the only son of an only son who could never return.

Twins

Christie 1994–2014

I failed to turn and walk away,
though my feet moved through the crowds
past the flowers and other gravestones
to where the car waited to take me home.

I remained, even after I'd gone,
staring at the granite and polished metal,
the gleam of black ice, the tire tracks
you left in someone's front yard, the unbuckled seatbelt.

I longed to hear the sound of your voice
call my name again, your laughter
light as a wind chime when you tell me about
the awkward moves of your latest would-be boyfriend.

I wanted to say that one last goodbye
like when you were first to leave
the ocean of the womb, cast out
into the artificial light of the delivery room.

I hoped the image of a church overflowing
with loved ones and your college friends would fade
back into two girls bouncing side by side in a playpen,
wearing matching outfits, so we could start over again.

But this landscape of bone is all I know now,
mausoleums of marble, winged statues without faces,
dusty holograms stirred by the wind where sometimes
I see your shadow following each step I take.

In Plain Sight

Why the swank hotel? The expensive liquor?
Why not on the cheap like a hitchhiker,
a transient, a freeloader? California dreaming

back to the Haight where everything was free,
and non-adult. Where nothing had consequences.
A little weed, a micro-dot of acid, a pill

to send you down the rabbit hole to Wonderland
where every girl was Alice rubbing her blondness
against your crotch. *Please be kind,* you wrote

from the desk in your room overlooking the whitecapped lake,
its beaten down pines. *There are so many things to forgive.*
How the words grew more stunted as you reached

back for the reasons, struggled with the apologies,
alcohol mixing with pain killers, until you were brave
enough to go forward. Cowardly enough

to do what you came here to do. Not the man
I knew, cocksure of everything in this world, answers
to every question, expert in all matters of the soul and love.

The search history on your computer revealed the alleyways
and tunnels your mind traversed. The ultimate solution,
how the plan was put together. *Please be kind,*

not something any of the characters in your novels would say.
From "no work, no food" mud-splattered Jamestown
to the tropical paradise of pre-white-man Hawaii.

They fought like wolves over what few spoils
existed in these worlds, willing to rip out the hearts
of anyone who got in their way. Not unlike the way you drove

your cab on the streets of New York, picking up dowagers,
Internet millionaires, or any bum flagging you down
as your brain silently pressed the keys on your keyboard

finishing the next line, skipping ahead to the next chapter.
The story within the story quietly progressed
beyond the smalltalk from the backseat

to rise above the façades of skyscrapers, into the clouds
and back through time to those places of fiction.
Please be kind, I hear you whisper, as the maid

found you hanged from the rafters, the coroner loosened the rope
and the crematorium flames sang their hymn of absolution.
Anonymous into this world, and anonymous out.

Leaving your loved ones to walk upon the ashes,
walk upon the body, behold your dark but lovely life
as a cedar broken into kindling by the wind,
their own lives unmanned without you.

Lynchburg Foundry, 1977

All it needed was Dante's inscription
above the entry gate. In my teenage stupidity,
I passed through with my hardhat tilted
in a backwards cool, the brim scrapping
the nape of my neck, lured by the exorbitant wage
of $5.50 an hour. The ninety degree summer day
melted into winter as I stepped into the smoke
and artificial lighting. The great blast furnaces gulped
their iron ore, limestone and coke
in a shower of orange plumes
more spectacular than any peacock.
I could see the heat radiating off of them,
even through the darkness, as the cloaked operators
moved the molten steel toward the assembly lines
where we made engine castings
for GM and Chrysler out of sand moldings.
Here there was no color or status; everyone was black
an hour into their shift from inhaling the smoke of burnt sand,
wading through its tides. Yet the foundry had an eerie allure,
a bewitching beauty that made me want to reach out
and touch the liquid steel, feel the sting
of sparks through my clothing, smell the singe
of flesh over the hiss and rush of flames all around.
My job was to shovel the sand that fell off
the conveyor belt as the castings traveled their slow path
to becoming a red hot solid, shovel what fell off of the shaker
as the molds were stripped away to reveal
the glowing orange heart of the engine,
and toss any loose scraps of metal onto the slag pile.
What circle of hell this was, no one knew,
or even dared ask the question. As the workers passed
their years here, they descended deeper and deeper,
from circle to circle, until black lung took them. I was in limbo,
yet could see the seven virtues shimmering through the smoke,
beckoning me to feel the sweat-soaked shiver of stepping out
into that end-of-August humidity one last time.
I still count my blessings by the burn marks on my arms.

The Lion of the Blue Ridge

after Rilke's Der Panther

The circus cage rotted slowly in the heat, a curious tourist
attraction parked beside Junior's Old Fashioned Country Store,
its Barnum & Bailey paint long since mouldered to grey.

Inside it, the lion of the Blue Ridge, defrocked from the big top,
his eyes dented and dull as the heavy silver coins
that changed hand inside to feed the economy.

What was it they saw as the arthritic paws paced
slow ovals around the rectangle of his imaginary
African plain? Mile after mile of bars encasing

a fortress of metal instead of the faces of the onlookers?
Or deer rustling through the brambles? His own footsteps
journeyed in ever smaller circles around the boundaries of his life,

the predator's will cowering before meals of butchered
cows and sheep. Yet occasionally when the powerful head
caught a stray scent on the breeze the nostrils would flare,

and for a fleeting moment his eyes filled with a blood-lust
that raised the hair on his back, exposed the dagger-like teeth,
extended the splintered claws for a quick kill

before it sputtered out, slipped back into darkness.
Then the wall of bars reappeared, the fumes of car exhaust,
that endless pacing, pacing, pacing
                                        longing for the taste of death.

Redneck Country

1. Elvis

No longer the Zen master of rock n roll
dressed in a rhinestone jumpsuit or black leather,
he now slings hash at *E's Hideway.*
The bikini-clad girls who danced
to the dreadful songs of his Hollywood movies
are nothing but a distant whiff
of sunscreen and cheap perfume.
Vegas is just a desert mirage
blooming into a cloud of dust kicked-up
behind the tailfins of a Cadillac heading east.
Into each stainless steel holder
he pushes napkins
as white as his mutton-chop sideburns.
He brushes his once raven-black hair
to the side as he refills
the salt and pepper shakers,
flashes a Buddha-like smile to Margaret,
the divorced waitress with two kids,
an alcoholic ex-husband and a face
beautiful enough to melt butter.
When he catches her looking at him
he sucks in his belly, pulls his shoulders back.
Later they'll have a good chuckle
back in the kitchen reading aloud the latest
Elvis sightings in the *National Enquirer.*
Sometimes at night in his double-wide
he finds himself drifting back
to his bad habits from the old times.
He fires a gun at his TV screen
waiting for the explosion
of electronics, the smell of burnt wire
and circuit boards that doesn't come,
then pulls the dart's rubber tip off the glass
and reloads. These rituals of loneliness
that hold his life together. Sometimes
he catches himself humming
Fools Rush In or *Heartbreak Hotel*
as he daydreams of a girl like his mother
who will love him for the nothing he's become,
the nothing he wants to remain

sitting in the dark behind a pair of sunglasses.

2. Norma Jean

Her platinum hair ripples in the wind
like a field of sunflowers
children could grow happy playing in.
But she has none of her own. She'll never
have any. Not with Joe, or Jack,
or Bobby, or even Arthur Miller.
They're all gone now, dead or estranged.
She lives alone with her pain blossoming
on the windowsill like an African violet.
The emptiness of her arms stretches
across the county's tobacco and corn fields,
its mines and sawmills to gather up
those who have no one else. They stand
before her desk at the orphanage
like starving birds, frightened,
teary-eyed, yet defiant and angry
as she takes down their names,
assigns them a dorm room, a guardian.
Under each head of unruly hair,
behind every runny nose
she sees her own face
passed from house to house,
from institution to institution, blown about
like a scrap of paper. After the near overdose
in the Hollywood hills, she disappeared
from the public, the parties,
the manic insecurity of fame mongers, died
to be reborn again among these kids.
She watches them play from her office window,
strolls the grounds and corridors
to touch their faces, hold their hands,
hug their lean bodies, hear the voices
of anguish and confusion grow into a mountain
that she is finally strong enough to climb on her own.

3. James

Grease rims the half-moon of his nails.
He leans against the back wall
of Jessie's Garage smoking,
uniform collar turned up, as he studies
the dark rivers flowing

through the relief map of his palms.
No pumice can scrub them clean.
No amount of lye or bleach.
They are the tattoos of his soul,
dark satellites the young girls
must embrace before he can touch them.
After the accident, his face is not quite so handsome,
more haggard, older, but the pain
still seeps through silent glances
like a plea for someone to save him
from himself. On a mechanic's salary
he's bought a red '55 corvette,
replaced the chrome, rebuilt the engine,
refurbished the interior. He cruises
the high school parking lots, attends
all the Friday night games, hangs out at the malls
and burger joints on the weekend.
He lures them with what's left of his looks,
his hair, the rebellious cool of his walk.
Then he shows them his hands,
places his fingers on their purity
to feel clean again for a moment. Dirty water
puddles in the streets around him. Birds swoop down
to drink the brown liquid. He watches,
lights another smoke, waits for the Chrysler's
oil to drain before he can plug it,
refill the reservoir. His fingertips
leave the smudge of their kiss
on everything they touch,
even the white label circling his name.

4. Cass

Each night at *The Sly Horse Saloon*
she sits by the jukebox. The glow
of blue neon transforms her
into a wild-haired oracle,
a soothsayer who can read each person's fate
in the songs they pick. No palm reading,
tea leaves or tarot. Her science relies
on the way the quarter spins
into the change box, the sound of buttons
being pressed, the singer's words,
the silences between notes, the intonation
of the voices. Truck drivers,

plow-boys, small-time Casanovas
saunter over to her for amusement
as she sits cross-legged on a stool,
cigarette smoke curling from her fingers
writing their futures in the air
in an alphabet only she can read.
They buy her beer after beer
to cloud her judgment, whirl
her around the dance floor
until the room spins like a six-side top,
and still she knows everything about them:
where they were born, how they'll die,
the fantasies alive inside their hidden lives.
Leaning against the bar, they call her
the "witch of the Wurlitzer," dare
the next victim to walk over jingling
their stack of quarters into a manhood
large enough to two-step their way into her heart.
Tapping her pack of cigarettes on the table,
she waits for the next one knowing
none of them will ever pick the right song
to go home with her tonight.

5. Jim

The Lizard King unzips,
writes his name in urine on the alley wall
as the bubble-top of a police car drifts by,
officers chatting, looking the other way.
Set free by the empty coffin that slipped
into the Paris ground, the maudlin tombstone
covered with graffiti, the life-size bust
surrounded by teary eyed pilgrims, he now roams
the streets in a green army surplus jacket,
Chuck Taylor tennis shoes, thrift store plaid
polyester pants, shoulder-length hair greasy and matted,
beard unevenly braided, a Rimbaud look in his eye.
Whatever words enter his mind escape
through the nozzle of a can of spray paint
onto the walls of the courthouse, the jail,
houses, schools, bridges, car hoods, and sidewalks—
any solid surface that can hold his stain.
Fragments of poetry, prophecy, scatology,
and word-pictures blossom randomly
around the city. A team of scrubbers follows

a day or two behind with cleansers and abrasives,
sanders and grinders, buckets of industrial paint.
In a walnut paneled office, the mayor fumes
over the overtime bills, slams his fist
against the wall. The police chief reads
the word *Pig* written repeatedly on the side
of his cruiser, kicks an Armor-alled tire in disgust.
Mr. Mojo Rising slinks from shadow to shadow,
crevice to crevice, crouches among the weeds
by the river, ducks through an opening
in the chain link fence into Bull Dog's Junk Yard.
He heads toward a blue Dodge Caravan
on the far side of the lot, front end totaled,
engine dropped, impact star on the windshield,
a makeshift bed laid out where the back seats
were removed. Cans of spray paint,
arranged by color, spiral around his eggshell mind
that dreams of dead Indians scattered on the highway,
the foot pressed on the gas pedal at the moment of collision,
and the wooden ark that bore him into this new life.

6. Janis

Whiskey a Go-Go, the Filmore,
the Summer of Love—now just dreams
crying out to be relived. Soberness
clings to her like a second skin, a veneer
that hides the little fat girl scarred by acne
who lives inside her. She needs a drink
of Southern Comfort, she needs a man,
she needs a hit of speed or smack,
but a paintbrush rests in one hand,
a cigarette in the other. The hills of Austin
or some other town stretch out before her,
echo onto the canvas in colors brighter than O'Keefe
as she sits in a lawn chair wearing a straw hat
beneath the shade of a beach umbrella
by the open trunk of her Rambler
filled with her paintings. She sells them
to the local galleries for half what they are worth
when she needs money, keeps moving
about the countryside in search of new scenes
as her voice damaged to a gravely whisper hums
along with the radio. Today, she faces a white
clapboard church tucked into a valley,

sees a dove rising from the steeple, the holy trinity
dwelling in the clouds above. Tomorrow,
it might be stripped mined mountains,
a river yellow as piss etching a path
through the runoff, the ghost smoke stacks
of power plants and steel mills looming
in the background where the coal once lay in strips
below the bedrock. The brush strokes are her songs,
pigments of emotion spilling over the canvas
as if she was still performing before crowds of thousands.
But the only applause she hears now
is the rustle of wind blowing through the trees,
slow, sustained, unlike anything else in her life.

The Birth of Faith Healing

Timber rattler,
when will I learn
how to hold you?

In the sunlight

I can't see your coils
nestled among straight pine needles
or the brown curl of last year's leaves,

but you sense my heat.

You feel me approach
loudly in boots
that long to unlace themselves,

feet that want to bathe

unfettered in mountain coolness,
touch all things cold and reckless,
the diamonds of your scales

gleaming like frosty stars to wish upon.

Through your pupils' vertical slits
faith falls all the way
from the Garden of Eden to here,

beside these rotting crab apples.

Your poison lies disguised,
a test of my beliefs,
to hold the devil

and his benediction of venom,

to drink the warm milk into my veins,
dream-deep the sleep of angels
and birth no child.

Buy the Ticket, Tame the Ride

quote from Hunter S. Thompson

Bible country. Protesters line
the road to the Super Wal-Mart
thrusting posters of bloody fetuses
at the cars passing by, babies
with heads caved in by the suction devices,
torsos torn in half by steel claws.

These are my people come
from the wilderness to smite evil. These
are my people moving through the desert
of their discontent past the golden calves
and statues of Ba'al to receive
the words born by Moses. These are my people
drinking from the spring in the rocks
where the staff struck, eating the manna of heaven.

I see them walking across
the parking lot, fathers and sons arm in arm,
dressed in worn jeans, glistening
as if they'd just stepped
out of the river with the holy spirit
dancing on their tongues.

In the produce aisle, they test
the bananas, the oranges
with hands hard as coal, soft as doves,
always on the lookout for anything
touched by the serpent.

A Kind of Weakness

Did this do anyone any good? I remember Blackwater Creek was up from the hurricane blowing through, the mud color water deep enough in some spots for swimming, but slow enough not to get swept away. We pretended to strip down to our skivvies, to God's beautiful flesh, and he, the fat boy, the butt of jokes, the slow one, beat us to it. Someone grabbed his clothes and took off running, holding them out like bait, as he pursued dressed in nothing but tennis shoes. It wasn't the grace of his run that captivated us, but the way he fell on the bank splitting his head open on the rocks, the blood that trickled between his clasped hands. It wasn't the way he put his clothes back on sobbing as we stood around making awkward apologies. It was the way he showed up at school the next day, stood in front of the class to get his picture taken, the purple scar on his brow matching the gold star on his perfect attendance certificate.

How to Fix Chilli in the Blue Ridge

First find a town too small to have its own Wal-Mart. There'll be a Piggly Wiggly or Acme store somewhere near Main Street. Grab a red plastic hand basket as you walk through the door. Buy a yellow onion, green bell pepper, cans of tomato sauce and kidney beans, Cactus Russ' 5-alarm mix, two large venison steaks from a deer shot with a bow, and a case of beer.

Almost seven in evening, pick up some Martha White corn meal, hum a few bars from their commercial. Drive your pickup out of town through the railroad crossing where the coal trains run until the pavement turns into a narrow tree-lined dirt road and static fills the radio and the cell phone loses its signal.

Within a circle of rocks on the mountain's western slope build a fire made of loblolly pine and white oak branches. Let it burn down to embers glowing redder than the sky. Place Gordo's dutch oven over the coals, add a little oil to the bottom, slice the meat up into fingernail size cubes. Toss the meat in, listen to it sizzle as you slice the vegetables up on a tin plate and open the cans with a hand opener.

As Al-dog says, char the meat brown as the soil. Watch the bottom of the pot blacken as you singe the hair on your knuckles stirring. Drizzle in a couple of beers instead of water, add the seasons, the vegetables, the contents of cans, mix as Gordo picks up his guitar and begins to strum a few John Prine songs.

Let it simmer with a heavy lid on top. Add water to the cornbread mix, whip with a fork until it looks like pancake batter, pour it into a frying pan that you clamp a lid on as you place it directly in the coals. Everything will be done in about 45 minutes.

Dish it out to your friends first, then take a seat on any rain-washed stump you can find. Dip your cornbread in the steaming red liquid, pause before taking a bite, let the spicy burn linger in your throat for a minute until it brings tears your eyes, then wash it down with a Miller Lite as an owl flies past the bloodshot eye of the moon.

Repeat again and again until your soul becomes a big-bellied cloud floating through the night sky.

History

only it never happened

I let the barn door stand open
so you'd think I was still inside
as the golden-eyed owl
flew across the meadow
clutching a mouse in its talons
and the cows moaned at milking time
like seasick sailors
leaning toward the sun-splash of mountains in the east

I climbed the ancient road
where canes of raspberries arched
in the mist like swords dappled with blood
ready to cut the tongue with flavor

below me where the brook
etched its path of charcoal through the valley
ruined farmhouses buckled
in tangles of undergrowth
the beams fallen together like hands
collapsed in prayer
a dark stain bruising
the fireplace where it curved like a cheek
and smoke fell across the shoulders
of the cedars
soft and fragrant as hair

what was it you sang
to yourself as your hands swished dishes
through the soapy basin
as your eyes fixed for too long on that distant horizon
or the rope tire-swing swaying in the wind
with no shoe prints around it

I wrote it all down
in longhand on sheets of notebook paper
day after day not like some portrait
at a fancy studio where they make you
into someone you'd always dreamed of
but hands at work a little dirt
under the fingernails a few cuts and scrapes
from digging blind potatoes out of the garden

I nailed it between the studs
in the barn 2x4s that I covered
with cedar wood so moths
wouldn't eat the words
we managed to do without
and blackened their wings with ink

so someone else might find it
when it's time to tear down and rebuild
to understand how we were wed
to this time and place
two bands of gold locked in above the knuckle
turning the fingertips purple

it was gone in the blink of an eye

Reassembling the Beast

see the tractor all gassed up and ready to go
reaping the curve of your eye
as oceans of wheat dip and roll in the breeze

listen to that watch you carry in your hip pocket
its wheels powered by the rhythm of your heart
the hands climbing and descending the rock face of time
urging you to get up and move

hear the winds blowing our children into the chinkapin
their feathers splayed against death
as the flood of moonlight
turns our lost roads into rivers rippling with fish

crunch them rocks underfoot
to knock the dust out of your ears
clear your muddled head
that puts miles between you and everything else

nail some roadkill to the fencepost
for the evil spirits to feast on
on the blackest of nights

but don't go round calling my name
or walk with your head sunk low like a sick dog
and expect me to come running

you know I don't cotton to no graveyard shovels
or sugar daddies who own half the county
with their women and their bourbon

now dig them nightcrawlers out of the earth
to thread the hook for the big cats
lulling in the darkest sinkholes

fix the clutch on our one-eyed Ford
replace that timing belt the cracked windshield
with its roadmap of spiderwebs

are there spare parts enough left to keep us running

your way of living is not worth wishing on anyone
that's why I'm here

With Malice Toward None

We ended where we began. By the Appomattox River,
we crossed over into civilianhood. Our grey coats,
nibbled by rats and shrapnel, eaten away by the blood

of our comrades, were not the only remnant we brought
of the horrors. Shadows followed us back
to the deserted cabin, where our parents lived before the war.

Azariah and I thought we knew how to do without them.
He remembered someone saying the hardest part
comes later when the bloodletting is over. But we laughed

it off as superstition. That damn fool Grant gave us back
everything but dignity as long as we promised
to walk back to our farms, start over, forget the battles.

Now we hunt rabbits instead of men, chop wood with axes
dull as bayonets, chase feral goats into makeshift pens
as if we were corralling prisoners. We start the same

march each day, traverse the same trampled grounds,
crisscross identical streams to circle back by nightfall
without finding any of our troops. What tricks the oil lamp

plays as the mind wanders over endless fields of bodies
where vultures roost in the trees waiting for evening,
unable to tell the difference between the dead

and the sleeping as darkness swoops down
with wings spread, head crimson as a fist
to beat us into unconsciousness. I believe

we can survive the body's wounds and suffering
just as we survived the slow unwinding of the war
from Petersburg to Amelia Courthouse to here

as our country's dream turned into smoke on the wind.
Brother, we are a creek that has flown back to its source.
A spring bubbling up from the ground

with nowhere to go. I am afraid of this peace
that brought us out of the ditches. Oh Lord,
change us back into something simple,

joyous, to be used in Thy service,
instead of two boys grown bitter on the ash
that flavors each morsel we raise to our lips.

Gladstone

Grey village of gravestones,
the dates are immaterial.

Skull of a church,
its eyes peering over landscapes
where dreams die back
to whatever gave them birth.

Intersection of railroad tracks,
sutures above
where something malignant
was removed.

It was here that it happened,
the great global geographies
distilled into a hieroglyphics
of cracked panes and window sills.

Here where it was born,
like a two-headed sheep
left to melt in the fly-swarm
of thistled fields.

And where it grew,
breastfed on stones,
hardened in the red
iron-fire glow of the forge.

There the first victims,
their names withheld,
met an anonymous ending,
endless pages of their lives left incomplete.

The story never stopped,
from the one room schoolhouse,
the clapboard shacks and farms,
the treachery, the guerrilla warfare of life.

It continued even after the bones
began to grow out of the earth,
seeds in this eternal springtime of death,
a crop that can never be harvested.

And then it rose up,

started coming after you.

What to Expect When You Become a Banjo

Whatever you were, now you're just wood, plastic and metal,
a field hand's distant dream of the Ivory Coast,
gourds and strings, the lonely wail of never going home again.

You pass your days in silence loafing against the wall,
daydreaming like a teenager, letting your hair grow long,
unkempt, slouching as you slowly drift out of tune.

Yet deep inside you long for the touch of the hands
that can raise you out of this stupor, make you sing
like a chorus of warped angels or the devil himself.

You feel finger rolls sending shivers up your spine,
the pinches letting out shrieks of harmony, the Scruggs style
slides, chokes and hammer-ons raising you to new heights of ecstasy.

Long gone are the days of blackfaced minstrels tap dancing
on the steps of Appomattox Courthouse while cartoonishly
strumming the five-string before cackling audiences.

Now you sing of coal trains chugging around bends,
wildwood flowers, mountain passes, lost loves, gospel roads,
and homesickness from the blue grass to the Blue Ridge.

Audiences cheer as each song ends, shout for more,
but you know you don't belong here. Your place is by the shacks
sprinkled around the tobacco and corn fields, or the isolated mountain

cabins where lonely men sit outside in rocking chairs
in the evening heat singing their songs of heartbreak and loss,
remembering the smell of cornbread and butterbeans on the table.

Finally exhausted by life's struggles, your voice hoarse,
strained, you lean against the wall, spend days in silent meditation
thinking of new ways to say: *I love you, I'll love you 'till the end.*

Family History

In this version of the myth
Niobe lost her own childhood,
not her children. Fate took

her father away in the middle
of the great depression, left
her mother impoverished,

relying on the ragged charity
of relatives for beans or collard greens
to fill six empty bellies that always

cried out for more. When kindness
ran its course, Niobe, her brothers
and sisters were dropped off

at the orphanage, where she quickly
became the mother of a hundred other
castoffs before she had her first period.

Each day there were breakfasts, lunches,
and dinners to make, rooms to clean,
clothes to darn and pass down,

cows to milk, butter to churn, cheese
to store and age, peanuts and potatoes
to lift from the earth, corn to shuck

for mouths that couldn't be filled.
The adults stood around, cruel and spiteful,
like gods who would devour their own offspring

to stay alive: men in bib overalls, chewing
blades of sweetgrass between their teeth,
as they threaten with pitchforks; women

in department store dresses, not a speck
of flour on them as they patrolled
the kitchen with steel serving spoons.

At night Niobe folded the two cotton
dresses she owned into funeral pillows
to view the white body of the girl

she used to be when she stepped through the gates.
She taught the others to do the same,
to worship the day of their dying.

They grew up by her side, nourished
in the strength of her example,
came of age and left to enter

an outside world filled with alcoholism,
crime, promiscuity, or a twisted
righteousness of purpose.

Eventually she too left to bear
her own children, watch them
blossom into adulthood, schooled

in the myth of her creation.
But with the repeated telling, their childhoods
began to visibly wither, compress

like coal into diamonds
that carved a channel of terrible beauty
wherever they traveled

waiting for the tears
which would not come
to fill their emptiness with meaning.

Eurydice

Don't believe what's been said.
It was Orpheus who died first.
His song faded as the daffodils

tolled like bells in the wind
announcing the arrival of spring.
While the days grew longer,

I cut my hair in mourning. It fell
in motes around the room, stirred
into flight by the slightest breeze

or footstep to sow my loneliness
throughout the house. His lyre lay silent
on the white bedspread between

pillows that still held the silhouettes
our profiles burned into the cloth
from our last night together

before he descended into a darkness
he didn't understand, and a different
kind of darkness encircled me.

But somewhere in those strings
his vibrations lingered; life beyond life
awaited the touch of my awakening.

I was not curious about love
when we first met, wasn't looking
for a husband to fill the house

with the cry of children. He took me
so easily into the world of troubadours
where there were gardens, balconies

and oaths of love to be sworn forever.
I barely knew what was happening.
as the tide of notes lifted him off the ground,

up to my window and into my arms
that opened like a night blooming flower
to the waters of the moon. But now I'm enslaved

by the feeling of my beauty being coaxed
into song, the rhythms that swell deep
inside when the music bathes me in its luster.

My fingers hesitate to touch the strings
of his lyre. They have become a gateway
to the twilight world that borders life and death.

Should we meet again in this dimness,
I'm uncertain if I could recognize him, or he me
in anything but the movement of his melodies.

Death has bleached his eyes with a truth
I cannot undo no matter how many tears
are shed as I replay his songs in my mind.

Prayers fold my body into ghost-hands
that reach out in blindness to touch
the steel of the strings. I absorb their vibrations

into my tendons, bones, and marrow
until my whole being resonates with
longing for his presence. My life has become a song

that calls him back from the caves
of the underworld to sing to me again
of how far he traveled for my love,

what he has sacrificed to worship
again at my feet. Even as the cold hand
of Persephone pulls him deeper, the hope grows

he will break free, follow my voice
through the glacial blueness of strings
that open into a birth canal to receive him.

Cerberus

He was the envy of all junkyard dogs,
his three serpented heads descending like hammers
to strike the leg of any intruder, extract
his pound of flesh, send them off screaming.

Yet most of the day he lay
on the front porch guarding the doorway of a house
whose hallways and staircases descended
into a netherworld where the tidal-basin

of the Styx lapped gently against docks,
and gondolas waited to ferry the dead
into a kind of darkness where the eternal fate
earned by the sum of their deeds awaited.

I can still smell the sulfur and bituminous oozing
beneath the doorway, seeping through cracks in the windows
as I pedaled by to toss the afternoon paper
beside his sleeping figure cloaked in chain-mail.

With the sudden plop he'd bolt upright,
fur stiff as porcupine bristles, blood pooling
in eyes that burned like mad orbs
to keep the breathing far from his master's kingdom

and tear after me as his massive paws
cleated the earth with unclipped nails,
so close I could see the loose strings of festering
flesh still worming between his bicuspids.

Then he'd jerk short as if an invisible rope were tied
to his spiked collar, turn, and trot back to his sentry post,
his tail, snipped and sharp as an adder's head,
waging with satisfaction at a job well-done.

I never witnessed the owner's pale hand open
the door to toss out a bone or fill his dish with food,
but my money was always sealed in an envelope
clipped to the mailbox, paid two weeks in advance.

News of the living and recently deceased
entered that house where nothing ever left—
no trash, no car in the driveway, or lawnmower

to cut grass that declined to grow beyond a dry stubble.

Just the great scary beast perched on the porch
like a sentinel, strands of slobber dangling from each
mouth as he surveilled the yard, cleaning himself,
tonguing that pink phallus erect with its barb and seed,

instinct driving him to seek out any bitch in heat
within a five mile radius. His horny midnight howls
stopped sleepers' hearts in mid-beat as he prowled
beneath their windows. His love was just another way of dying.

Jefferson and the Love Apple

The tree of liberty must be refreshed from time to time
with the blood of patriots and tyrants.
— Thomas Jefferson

Before the debate between Heart and Mind
in the letter to Maria Cosway, the sage
of Monticello, the squire of Poplar Forest,
not yet the chaste widower

absorbed in a lifetime of mourning,
stood in this very spot on the streets
of my hometown with his loose red hair
lifting and falling in the breeze like a Continental flag.

The ink from the Declaration of Independence
was still wet on his fingertips, and his multi-terraced intellect
grew in fevered pitches and starts like his gardens
on the Charlottesville mountainside, or the house itself.

He stood where I stand in the Virginia sunshine
as the dream of the great American experiment
blossomed all around, and conversed with friends
while his horse whinnied and stirred the dirt beside him.

But inside as he talked his Heart did not plead
for him to give into impulse and instinct,
expose himself to the hurt and rejection of love,
or the even more frightening—acceptance.

Nor did his Mind caution to remain withdrawn,
calculated, distant enough to maintain
the proper philosophical detachment
as taught by his Greek masters.

Those voices slumbered within waiting for their day and time.
He only heard the sound of his own voice
when against conventional wisdom he reached out
and plucked a fruit from the wild vine.

The warm red skin with its pulp and seeds
fit into his hand as firm as a nubile breast,
the faintly raised nipple on the end
awaiting the caress of his lips. He fondled

54

it with his fingers, alternating between teasing,
denial and saturation when at the moment of ecstasy
he raised it to his mouth, took a bite,
and red juice dripped down his chin onto the soil.

Its poison entered his veins like a kind of freedom.
His friends, panicked that he would lose his life,
ran to summon the doctor to begin the blood-letting
but it had already begun as he rode away.

The Doll

His toys lie scattered around him like so much flot-sam in the middle of the room. Fire engines, race-cars, video games, music CDs, headphones. None of them hold his interest. He surrounds himself with action figures, flesh-colored dolls a little larger than an adult hand. They have bendable joints, come out of the box dressed in fatigues with stern faces. He calls them his troop, has named the unit Desert Jackal, and invented a battle cry for them that would raise fear in all but the most righteous. From central command, he leads them on missions of reconnaissance, night raids, and terror-ist hunts. Complicated missions that require intricate planning, intense focus, almost the delicate choreogra-phy of a ballet. His men are outfitted with the latest equipment—night vision goggles, body armor, rapid-fire guns. They walk through fields of land mines, alleys of snipers, streets where any vehicle or pedestrian could conceal a bomb. I hear his mouth making the noises of machine gun, mortars exploding, tanks firing rounds into buildings. But each time the group returns whole. No injuries, no casualties. Yet I notice one stands apart; one of them cannot go out on the missions. He lies on the carpet dressed only in green military boxers. His face is colored blue with magic marker. The boy says: "I don't think anyone can help bring him back, not God or Allah. But he's not dead. He just can't move. He can't get up and join the others." I see the yellow coloring on its arms, chest and legs; the hands painted red, the bottom of the feet. Faint gurgling sounds rise from the throat. Not sobs or weeping or trembling with fear. But a rushing of water from far off, as if a canyon was being carved out by a voice that can no longer speak. Even as his comrades joke and laugh, drink, dance in between missions, they live with the knowledge his fate does not await them; that this is just pretend and his living *rigor mortis* will not spread into their joints. But when the boy leaves the room, when there is nothing but their own quietness to stare into, the blue soldier's agony unfurls like a flag over this landscape.

Biograph Theater

You are the cigarette dangling from pursed lips, and I,
I am the match that flares to illuminate your features,
shadows your profile into deeper nuance
until the mystery that is hidden behind layers of mascara
flakes down like ash to soften this black and white shot.
The director zooms the camera lens in tighter to capture
this smoke that questions our being, the kiss of lipstick,
the breath now visibly flowing between us, shared
like bootlegged liquor. I don't know if you're the secret
of secrets, the one who has no name, the words my soul
burnt itself up to hear. You smell like a rose plucked
from the barrel of a Tommy gun, so dirty only fire
can make you clean. I bring you my drop of blood,
my tear of sulfur, all the hurt one life can muster.
My body is left spent on the sidewalk, the glow dimming
in my eyes as you slip through the gathering crowd,
and your red dress fades into a darker grey before the camera
pans out and there's no one left to follow you into history.

Why Jimmy Can't Read

His head bent low over the page,
the words squirm before him like ants
stirred into anger by his finger,
black squiggles turning red,
as he struggles to decipher
their meanings, mouth their sounds.

It's not like he poured gas
into their nest and set it on fire
or dug up all their tunnels.
So why should they swarm
over his body, pincers biting,
making him itchy and fidgety
as he is pelted by his classmates' laughter.

Hitting a curve ball or slider—
so much easier than sounding out
Clemente, Killabrew, Concepcion,
even with phonics and flashcards.
And snagging a long fly over the shoulder,
spinning to make the perfect throw
to second to nail the runner—
peanuts compared
to deciphering the sports page.

Now the whack
of a ruler on his neck
sends the words scurrying off
The teacher calls him *slacker, class clown.*
The time spent after school
sponging blackboards, dusting chalk
from the erasers is his revenge
as he scrubs all traces
of these letters from his life.

To Serve Beauty

I live a truly simple life,
eat brown rice everyday, sit in my cabin
at the edge of the woods like a scholar
in a Chinese painting. Only a few brush strokes
are necessary to position me beneath
the gnarled branches of a white pine
as the mist rises from a waterfall
up the sheer mountain cliffs,
a third of the canvas left incomplete
on purpose. Missing is the square
of garden in the back whose perimeter
shrinks a little more each year
like my cataracted vision, the bedroom
twice as wide as a single bed,
the hearth made of native stone,
the wooden box that doubles
as a refrigerator in winter,
and the scraps of paper filled
with scribbles that surround me
as I embrace denial, my mistress.

And the guy holding the brush,
who is he but my shadow,
my antithesis? His waxed mustache
and oiled hair glow in the sunlight,
the pallet of colors more plentiful
than I am capable of imagining
from my world of blacks, browns and greens,
the canvas yellowed with age. Through binoculars
I watch him fill in the details
of my mountain, switching from one
size brush to another. Then I walk down
to where he works, invite him
to a dinner of potatoes, wild greens,
a few sips of dandelion wine.
Before a roaring fire his false English
accent falls like ashes through the grate
and all I'm left with is the outline
of a person struggling to figure out
where his mind wants to take him,
all his hues whisked away by the wind.

Impressionism

clouds hang low
over a city
weighed down by the burden
of untold centuries

all roads lead
to and from the factories

the rain falls grey upon the pavement

the ocean rolls steel-colored
onto the pebbled shore
where the dinghies
lay overturned

then from the drabness
your children step forward

one in vibrant orange
the other in cheerful yellow
beside the pond
with its blooming water lilies

Gratify

In Magritte's painting *Plagiarism*
art refuses to imitate life, twisting and bending
perception into a new, deeper reality.

Your own world remains flat, pre-Columbian,
with monsters and precipitous drop-offs
on either side of sunrise and sunset,

not a globe trampled by irresponsible children
who backpack off to other countries
on their parent's nickel.

The rooms are filled with the songs
of finches, their nests cut out
from the wallpaper, filled with eggs,

as they glean the carpet for seeds,
hop through tree limbs, build a life
for themselves within these boundaries.

What blooms on the table blooms inside
the mind, as well as outside these walls,
each mirroring the other's reality.

You can smell the musk
of the damp soil of spring,
feel the pollen irritating your nostrils,

and this art is undefinable, though you leave
your prints all over it, allergic to the beauty,
savoring it every chance you get, alone.

Letter to Lyne in Lafayette

Dear Sandy:
the first warm breath of spring, even in the midst
of winter, takes me back to our days in Charlottesville
when we'd stroll around the university grounds, surrounded
by visions of Jeffersonian order—serpentine walls,
Palladian windows, whitewashed columns, symmetry
in every detail— as we discussed Lorca, Neruda, Jiménez,
Ekelöf, Transtromer, to name a few, and Rimbaud's
systematic derangement of the senses, too timid
to actually try it on ourselves, but intrigued
by the idea. We strolled along the tidy boulevards
between the Pavilions with their well-mannered gardens,
flower beds and espaliered fruit trees like novices
dressed in the cloaks of our prelates. Bedlam
embraced the world around us: the resignation
of Nixon, the fall of Saigon, Ayatollahs creeping out
of sand dunes to take hostages and dry up
the flow of oil to the pumps. We were enthralled
by the chaos of creation, inventing our own primeval
worlds, painted in the torchlight of our souls
as we unearthed pained mythologies. Yet years have passed,
distances, lifetimes. The blue moon of Kentucky
has become a ragin' Cajun, a Zydeco dancing machine,
while I remain the stiff-collared corporate citizen
living a secret double life, and somehow we're still poets.
You more so than me, with your students and books,
your readings around the country. Now I hear the word cancer
mentioned along with your name. Esophageal.
In the advanced stages, requiring full reconstruction.
This different kind of chaos, where the body rebels
against itself. And the country continues to go to hell
all around us: the Iraq war, Hurricane Katrina,
the incompetence of bureaucrats. Refugees
flock to your city, including the doctor from New Orleans,
better than the best, who currently has your case
by some strange twist of fortune. Payback for your rare
good deeds performed there before the flood waters receded.
Yes, my friend, there is a God who occasionally remembers
those brought here to make the world a better place.
Keep reading your Rolf Jacobsen. The miracles will never cease.

Love, Jim

Letter to Martin from Fincastle

Dear Hugh:
here the cows must outnumber the people 1000 to 1.
The farms stretch like a warm blanket around the center
of town, anchored by its courthouse and jail,
and churches that crowd forward for attention. Every Wednesday
evening and Sunday morning the people knock the cow dung
off their boots, scrape the engine oil from under their fingernails,
splash on a little dime-store cologne or perfume, slick
their hair back and sit with folded hands to hear
about the rapture, when all souls ascend to heaven
to be one with Jesus in their immortal bodies. No doubt
the libs and sophisticates would get a good chuckle
over these simple people who grasp your hand firmly,
look you square in the eye with an ah shucks grin
on their faces, and the global warmers have a field day
calculating all the methane released from each end
by these acres and acres of cud-chewers. Somehow, I feel
at home among these people, though they treat newcomers
with guarded suspicion, but eventually their southern
hospitality takes over and they are inviting you over
for a dinner of fried chicken, biscuits and gravy,
riding you on their tractors from one end of the farm
to the other to tell you about crop rotation,
pasture lands, hay fields, water sources and maybe
share a nip of moonshine hidden in the loft of the barn
furthest from the house. The River Jordan cuts
through each track of land, and what I wouldn't give
to bathe in its waters and be cleansed, set free.
The day your three year old son drowned in a neighbor's pool
I lay unconscious on an operating table.
Your telephone call came through the haze of anesthesia.
I don't remember the exact words, just the message,
my inability to travel, to be with you at the funeral.
My shame, built brick by brick, like the Wailing Wall,
to stand isolated in time. I found the grave on a lone hillside
in the family plot. The polished stone reflected my image
and the sky behind in the finality of its carved letters.
I stood there in silence, waiting for the rapture,
the ark to lift from the earth to carry us heavenward,
the dead and the dying as one. For hours nothing happened.
The sky became graphite around me, then obsidian.

The firmament above still separated heaven and earth.
Nothing had changed. Forgive me, who can't forgive myself.

Forever your,
Jim

Your Green Dream

You're lost amid the moss again.
It drips from trees in antebellum curls.
Even beaded with rain, it feels dry
in your hands, a kind of ripcord,
that whispers "north, this way is north,"
and like a compass needle you bull through
the undergrowth, move parallel to the lengthening
shadows as soft whips strike your face,
arms, and legs. The taste of blood
paints your lips from a roadmap of cuts.

You break through into the clearing
and startle a family just pitching their tent.
The little girl wants to scream
when she sees you, but is shuffled
behind her mother. Which way to town?
They don't answer. Their eyes stare back
round as toadstools, but the gravel road
is full of fishermen heading somewhere.
Their rods bend like saplings over their shoulders
as if they've hooked the big one. Yet the only
thing out here that might bite are the clouds
which scuttle after them on centipede feet.
You follow, asking the time, the day. Again
silence. Your memory grows dimmer
as evening approaches. To hell with them.

In darkness you run across a lake
toward the shimmering city, your shoes
dry as Jesus' sandals, your pants cuffs ringed
with water. You zigzag through the numbered
city streets until you stand before a battered
door with a lion's head knocker. A redhead
answers the door and hands you a bowling ball,
says you don't live here any more. A pack
of bloodhounds bays in the distance sniffing
out your trail. The sheriff's posse is after you,
and all you can do is yell out: Where's my home?

The moon tries to answer with a mouthful
of clover, but all you hear is the whine
of the wind pointing east. You strap your belt

to it, hitch a ride to the nearest carnival.
The lights of the arcade blind you, but there's
no one here but the workers. You're dressed
in top-hat and tails, everyone else is in rags.
They stare at you like you're royalty,
but, instead of bowing, shout: "Go home,
you dirty dog, go back to your own land."
They throw dirt clods and rocks. You scream:
"but where is my home, where is home?" To the south.

The south. The stars are fireworks in the sky.
You follow the brightest explosion, slogging
through knee-high weeds and moths that flutter up
only to be scorched in the candle of the moon.
Their spent bodies drift down like dirty snow.
A platoon runs past you on a night march.
The sergeant kicks your ass as if you were a Pfc.
You join their ranks in the rear dressed in your fatigues,
a name that isn't yours written in magic-marker
across your chest, a rifle that isn't yours
white-knuckling your hands. They are all
running toward a green elephant that suddenly
opens its jaws to turn into a cargo plane. Inside, the walls
are covered with centerfolds. One by one
the engines drone, shredding the hairy moss
that covers the propellers. The moon
casts a cyclopean eye over all winged creatures.

You rise into the blackness, defying the laws
of physics, knees knocking together,
helmet clanking against the hull. Then the door
opens, and you are spit out into nothingness
like a BB, a cluster bomb, a tomahawk missile
that slices through the air still searching for home,
programmed like a dog to find it, circling, circling,
until you parachute, roaring, into that bonfire.

A Letter to Jerry Falwell from Liberty Mountain

Dear Jerry:
I can still remember when this was called Candler's Mountain.
Back then there were just trees and a signal relay station
with its orange and white antennae pointed at God's blue sky.
Before that a guano factory stuffed burlap sacks full
of the same kind of fertilizer many accused you
of spouting in front of the microphones,
and the Odd Fellows Home dispensed its brand
of charity to my mother and other area orphans.

Both buildings are gone now, demolished
by the wrecking ball, save for a few souvenirs
collected by those to whom these places held special memories.
You came from a gas station on Campbell Avenue—
the bootlegger's son, fratricide staining
your father's hands—to raise the Bible over the heads
of a handful of believers who first met in the abandoned
Pepsi bottling plant, over hundreds in the sanctuary
of Thomas Road Baptist Church, then thousands
first in black and white. then color,
on the TV show The Old Time Gospel Hour.

You were the lawgiver, the blue-suited voice
bellowing from the pulpit as if your brain
was tethered to the Lord's bellybutton,
the conscience of a new morality awakening
like Eve's first blush in the Garden of Eden.
You urged your congregation to interpret
each scripture literally, embrace the contradictions
and codify to the least common denominator.
Whether David or Goliath, you picked your battles haphazardly,
relied on your Savior to guide your words like stones
and spears to your opponent's most vulnerable places.

This morning when God took you from the earth,
your heart too large to keep on beating,
like a star collapsing into its own gravity,
the TV networks paused their regular programming.
Vitriol and hatred filled the airwaves as your detractors
practiced what they accused you of preaching,
politics and religion mixed like Molotov cocktails
into a series of drive-by firebombings, no concern for casualties.

Fed up, I drove to the top of this mountain
where you built your shining city, a University of disciples
to spread the Gospel to the four corners of the world.
Some might say that backlit by a sunset it could pass
for a little bit of heaven. But who has any real
idea what heaven looks like?

And as I gaze down on a modern day city of seven hills,
what you've set in motion doesn't stop with the death
of one man, the charities, the unreported good deeds
for the poor and faithless, many of whom cursed you
under their breath as they accepted your aid. Rest assured,
the work goes on. Those same people who stopped me
years ago in the bus stations or shopping malls
trying to save my soul from eternal torment are still out there.
They knock on doors, run shelters and detox centers,
feed the hungry, always looking
for new converts to spread The Word.

The Dosses and the Falwells knew each other well enough
across the generations to understand that neither family
raised any saints—just more than our share
of stubborn, opinionated people. So wherever you're at now—
the hell of the left or the paradise of the right—save a place
for me. I won't be far behind.

Jim

Jedem das Seine

after William Heyen

Herr Doktor,
Ich heisse Klara Kirsche, KZ Buchenwald.
I enter your imagination now
of my own free will to speak a few words
after what seems like light years of circling
the sun and stars. *Kirsche*—yes, cherry—
and as a child I loved *Schwarzwälder Kirschtorte*
made by my mother's delicately strong hands
and sprinkled with chocolate and a pinch
of red from my cheeks. Cherries
covered the tree beside the dirt road on Ettersberg
where I led the young women to the armaments factory,
and somewhere in each of us was a small bird
leaping through the limbs to eat our fill.
None of us thought of the *Goethe Eich* inside the gate,
Verkörperung des deutschen Geistes,
in whose shade he wrote his masterpieces.
We were instruments of war, that was our fate,
tattooed numbers, hands that worked machines
to make the red flow brighter in another land
as we dreamed of Zion, the Palestine of legend.
I hoped for any victory, *Herr Doktor,*
was that wrong? I pushed myself and those girls
for a *Reich* that sought their god in the snarl
of a German shepherd, the smile of a radiant blonde youth.
We wrote our stories in the invisible ink
of the weight we lost, our arms turning into branches,
our fingers becoming twigs. Think of us
in the spring as the cherry blossoms fall
so beautiful and delicate
and later when the sweetness of the fruit
touches your tongue with our destiny.

Homage to Ezra

Of all the poses, of all the voices,
which one will you keep?
Does anything still tether you to Idaho
or Pennsylvania, where flags clothesline
the breeze? American tanks and jeeps
thunderhead into cities as gondola oars
stir the dark canals of night
like fingers of moonlight.
Under different circumstances
you'd read your fortune in the ripples
of the boats sliding through the darkness,
but today they look like coffins
moving the bones of an old empire
to a clandestine crypt. Usury, central bankers
printing money out of thin air, the corruption
of democracy as they infiltrated government
and bought support for the war from the media outlets—
you railed against it all in your radio
broadcasts supporting Mussolini, the Axis powers.
Now you turn yourself in only to have
the occupying authorities letter you mad
as you hawk above them riding the thermals
of their words. What do they know about poetics
or economics? Caged behind steel bars,
yet teased by sunlight and wind, you dream
of Ithaca, the return home, the feathers
used to fashion arrows for the suitors
and end another kind of treason.

In Another Life

East Berlin

There were many frontiers to be crossed,
some imaginary, some real. I wrote so boldly
there that my words had no choice but to scatter

like cockroaches before the boots of the censors,
scrambling under baseboards, through heating vents,
into light fixtures. They passed unnoticed

through the cemeteries of buildings, cars, sidewalks
and citizens who walked like upright tombstones
with carved gargoyle faces freckled with moss.

What couldn't be said swelled between
the peoples' sternness like a thousand Hindenburgs,
each awaiting the spark of a machine gun burst.

Checkpoint Charlie was little more
than a one-armed bandit for all those
Peter Fechters ready to risk their lives

for the jackpot of bourgeois freedom. How often
I dreamed of walking through the charred
and bullet riddled skeleton of the Brandenburg Gate

past the guard towers, razor wire,and gnashing teeth
of German Shepherds toward that other prison
just on the opposite side of the wall

where people were constrained only by their intellect
and ambition. My prison was my room, a place of sanctuary,
hidden from those who still believed

Arbeit macht frei, their microphones
listening within the walls for any subversive whisper.
What they couldn't hear was the pen moving

across paper, my thoughts written in invisible ink,
deconstructing their prison bar by bar
to gladly build my own with its winding staircase

descending to that hell where I speak truth to power
between the barbs and stings of demons. *Folgen Sie mir,*

mein Freund. Our fate cannot be taken from us.

el lector

Somedays I believed I could be Teddy Roosevelt
riding high in the saddle
charging the hills of San Juan.
But what was there to conquer?
I lived my life amid the smells of loose
leaf tobacco, sweat, salsa, and *ropa vieja*,
the bodies fallen around me as I liberated
the mind from the tedium of hands
rolling cigars for the wealthy
gentlemen of the south,
or the dandies in New York City.

Swords of light pierced the dust
to turn brown skin browner, and carve furrows
of worry into the *sueño americano*
of Ybor City. My voice from the *tribuna*
chipped through their boredom
like the hammering of a chisel,
planting word-seeds into brains
teeming for stimulation.

Les Miserables was a favorite
as the escaped convict Jean Valjean
outwitted Javert and showed that those who sacrificed
themselves could indeed help the pure of heart
inherit life's bounty, anything about the workers
or the poor triumphing over the rich owners
or the propaganda rags trumpeting out
their calls for the laborers to rise up
and overthrow the exploiters.

But most times when I looked down
over the corner of my book or newspaper,
all I could see were the meek faces of Jesus' poor,
the stone statues of unknown martyrs
sacrificing themselves to a dream of a better
tomorrow for their children and grandchild.
The boiling blood of revolutionaries
remained festering in their home countries.
We were all *yanquis* now, and I gladly
accepted their pooled monies
to play god, politician, hero or heroine

on any given day to avoid the calluses,
the tobacco stains, the squint-eyed monotony
of taking a job below my designated station in life.

Vivaldi's *The Seasons*

It was as if winter
were suddenly born from their coupling.

The first snows of the season
swirled about his head
as he steped from her apartment
out onto the street.

The afternoon shown white
like the inside of a cathedral whose stained-glass
was slowly disappearing
in a radiance he couldn't understand.

The deserted sidewalk led back
to the office where no-one
would question the wetness of his hair,
the moisture striping
his coat's shoulders like epaulets,
or the unreturned
phone calls from home.

As he walked, all the flakes
falling from the sky
swirled together
to become notes on sheet music
and sang to him of God's being.

The choir of questions
that plagued his life
raised their voices upward
from this world cloaked in white.

Music broke out on his lips
in rhythm with the crunch of his shoes
on the snow covered sidewalk. At the corner
of Euclid and Third he turned left

instead of right, strolled along
the tree-lined edge of the river
as the street lamps were coming on.
The melody swept him up

into the air, through

thousands of tiny branches
where there was just enough breathing
space for a man to meet his angel.

To Werner in Trier

As if in a dream
You turn to the calm lamp within.
   – Georg Trakl

Trakl's autumn is upon us and like righteous pilgrims
we struggle to translate his poems.

Nouns blow in from the woods to nestle
against our doors, collect in porch corners.
Adjectives rattle inside of dried seed pods.
Crystalline verbs cling to brown blades of grass
and like ghosts live longest in the shadows.

My footsteps sing out crossing fields of stubble corn
as the wind carries the air
I breathed yesterday across the ocean
to become the oxygen that reddens
the blood of the words that pass between us today.

Each syllable is a feather
I use to reconstruct the hawk's body
missing from the wings
I discovered outspread at the edge of the field.

I raise the bloody stumps like a lyre
to hear the voice of the wind. I fix the sockets
into my shoulder blades, ride the air currents back
to the old country where I see you standing
in the shadows of Black Gate holding a black cat.

I soar over the three ponds of Hellbrunn
to the gothic splendor of the beautiful city,
climb the slopes of the Mönchsberg,
storm the turrets of fortress Hohensalzburg.

On either side of the Atlantic
we turn his words into purple candle flames
that light darkened rooms
as our heads slowly silver
with the winter wisdom of the lonely one.

Thinking of No. 263 Prinsengracht, Amsterdam on November 10, 1953

Dear Diary,

These words have always haunted me: *At the proper temperature,
the body is engulfed by flames, and becomes a flame itself
colored with the blues, greens and oranges of the spirit as the soul
is released to rise as cinders through the heat of the ovens.*

I can't remember who wrote them anymore. But I know
I never read them in the Talmud or even the Nazi Book of Cruelty,
just in the eyes of the guards, their uniforms
greyed with soot, the char they still cannot wash from their skin.

Shortly after Anne's words were translated into German
their letters of apology began to arrive begging a kind of forgiveness
I can only give on this earth, but not eternally, their faces so young
like façades just starting to weather trying to hide a lifetime of guilt.

How can I explain grief to them, these boys who believed
the Füher's big lie as they exterminated grandparents
and children who might have been their playmates in a better age
where automobiles were manufactured instead of tanks?

The emptiness of family and friends gone forever,
the heaviness of my heart like an anvil upon which I must
reforge myself each day, even today when I am to wed
Elfrei, another Survivor from our old neighborhood.

It's strange, but on my afternoon walk I overheard someone
leaving a café remark on the unseasonable snow drifting down
from dreary clouds, how each unique flake was a star shedding
its skin to touch us with magic for one brief moment,

not the six-sided kind like those sewn on the camp uniforms,
but the five-sided ones painted on religious icons in churches.
Yet deep down I knew it was really Margot and Anne
wetting my cheeks with their kisses to tell me everything was ok,

just like when they'd arrive home safely from school
to catch me napping in my chair, the girls eager to brag
once again about how they bested their classmates
on the examinations. Each snowflake and raindrop brings

a small part of them back to me to be sealed away again
behind bookcases in those surreptitious rooms, the walls collaged
with pictures of Robert Taylor, Marlene Dietrich, the royal family
in exile, and a map with stick pins plotting the Allied advance.

This place where no harm can come in spite of informants
and the SS who never truly penetrated this sanctuary no matter
how many muddy boots tramped through the hidden doorway.
May we always find some reason to embrace the joy in this world,

Otto

Eisenstaedt's Photograph of Robert Frost
at His Desk

His hair, already ruffled
by the snowy wind of his thought,
sways as another idea blows past.

In his farmhouse study
out of camera-view
a pencil scrawls across paper.

His words absorb the shape
and texture of the wood grain in his desk.

They sprout leaves,
dream about growing
into trees and thickets, birches
whose white branches are thick
enough for a boy to build a swing on
or ice splinter into next year's firewood.

But his desk is no desk at all,
just a loose strip of plywood
sawed to fit lap and chair,
jerry-rigged to the perfect writing angle
by an oak branch he cut and trimmed
with a pocketknife on one of his walks.

Yankee frugality is etched
into the very lines of his face,
the soles of his canvas shoes,
the simple painting hung on a nail
and the self-upholstered chair.

Yet his hands, busily hidden,
are mending walls of weathered stone
to keep us off of his property,
ensure we remain good neighbors,
as he heads further down
the road less travelled.

The House of Pestilence, Lynchburg

The Honorable Joseph Virginius Bidgood

June 1, 1865

Dear Sir,

Three railroads blessed my town with their intersection.
The battles mapped a broad circle around us,
and the wounded poured in by the thousands,
as if they were locust descending on Egypt's grain fields.
Hotels, private residences, the tobacco warehouses
were transformed into hospitals. Anyone with a conjurer's
knowledge of medicine was handed a bone saw
and a bottle of chloroform. At pistol point

I involuntarily enlisted in the Confederate Medical Corp.
At no time did I wear the uniform or honor
the rank. I was there for the men, to ease their suffering.
The worst were sent to the Pest House, which boarded
smallpox victims before the war. It had a graveyard
on one side, on the other a stable filled
with the quartermaster's glanders, and mortality
always on the mind like a dream of deliverance.

I talked the painter into whitewashing the outside
of the building with lime for purity, then covering
the clapboard with the colors of the rising sun.
Black was reserved for the inside to shelter their eyes
from any harsh thoughts or disturbing images. I sprinkled
the floor with a white sand, watered it down each morning
and evening to overcome the odors of rot and death.

For the open wounds and nerve ganglia, a bucket
of lime mixed with linseed oil was used as ointment
to grease the wounds, deaden the pain
and keep the bedclothes from sticking.
Humane or not, it served its purpose
and made the heat of high noon more tolerable,
kept the flies from laying eggs on the bloody stumps,
the hatchlings from feasting on flesh.

There are no heroes anywhere, only survivors. I felt
their heartbeats daily, strong or weak, warmed my fingers

on their fevers. For a time the saw became my life,
used my hands for its own purpose as if I was walking
a dirt road filled with dead beetles. the crunch of their bodies
all my ears could hear. Even after the surrender,
the men stayed on, clinging to any hope, any surge
of strength that might raise them from the bed.

Given that I've now doctored all my patients
either into the grave, or whatever semblance of good
health they can muster, limbs missing, consumptive,
orphaned from their families, sodden with drink,
I hereby resign my position from whatever authority
now commands me to return home to *Rock Castle*,
my farm in Campbell County, without a cent to my name
to begin the civilized practice of medicine.

Sincerely,
Dr. John Jay Terrell

Jamestown

The past five months of horror at sea
gives way to this horror of wilderness
bordering the ragged Virginia shoreline,
while the mosquito wings of fever carry people
through burning bushes no one else can see.

Bodies float through the wooden
gates of our fort on stretchers
made of trimmed poles and heavy
curtains brought here from England
that double as shrouds.

They meet their maker face-up,
eyes left open to receive the light
as their souls enter paradise
and each shovelful of dirt
concealed our misery from their view.

The dandified gentlemen who came
here for easy money—gold, spices,
the passage to the Orient—sit on dainty
furniture playing cards, betting sea shells,
beads and pouches filled with tobacco.

What few holes they dug before tiring
fill with swamp water, fester like sores,
green into a broth that teems
with insect larvae twitching into flight
to infect those not already infected.

No one's naked arms or legs are exposed
to the poisonous air with its smells of sulfur
that conjure up the realities of hell
as real as any story Dante might dream up
resting between the perfumed breasts of his beloved.

What soldiers can still be commanded
clear a field in full armor, hack down
trees and underbrush with swords
and axes, prepare the soil for peas,
broccoli, maize and pumpkins.

The eyes of the forest, more animal

than human, watch our movements
with the curiosity of feral children
who can't be satisfied until they tame
the magic of our strange ways.

I carry a black leather-bound book
with me into the fields for protection,
read the words aloud from a recently
printed King James version over the bowed
heads of my fellow sufferers struggling to survive.

With the ships departed on the voyage back
and their return uncertain, we are abandoned
to invent our own religion, our own creed
in this land we must first turn into bread and wine
before we commit the sin of desiring too much.

Le charme discret de la bourgeoisie

How did I come to exist in faded color
between the frames of a Buñuel movie?
Here the peasants are so well hidden they can't
even be seen much less heard protesting over wages.

When I look out the window the grass seems
to roll on forever like the swells of a placid lake
that hunger for footsteps. The hedges never need
trimming and the wind barely stirs a leaf.

The pool suns itself out back immaculately
unused, the tennis court a little beyond that.
Soft as a whisper I close the curtain to see
its print of vineyards and grape cutters
holding knives with blades hooked
like a hawk's beak before I retreat to watch
the price of stocks move up and down.

China and silverware sparkle as if new
on the table where delicacies always appear
at the appointed hour. I observe my grey veined
hand reaching out to grasp the cold hand
of my wife as I lead her to her chair.

But only in dreams do I live—
a woodcarver's apprentice sneaking out
at lunchtime to make love to the master's wife.

A Thanksgiving Poem from Lemondrop Johnson

The blues is like a dog gone mean from lack of tenderness.

For seven hard years I worked
the plantation of her love,
chipped away at the hardpan,
felled trees to clear new fields.

More than my share.

Deep in summer when the mosquitoes
were the size of hummingbirds,
I wrapped stumps with a logging chain,
spun comet trials of dust
with my tires,
courted her with crowbar
in hand as she and her friends
drank lemonade in a gazebo
by our trickle of a river.

I went halves on everything with her,
sharecropping her soul,
dreams and night sweats,
the trout leaping up to kiss the moon,
cotton plants raising their shriveled clouds
up to the sky for rain.

Her bedroom was a trembling bridge
no man would dare cross uninvited
as she sat in front of her mirror
brushing waterfalls of hair,
or looking at the bee
inside the rose crushed
between the leaves
of the family Bible,
those names written in longhand
who had long since passed into backwater.

And here I am now,
with snow nipping at my ankles,
a cigarette
burning back through the years,
smoke, beer, a wall on which I lean.

My nights are spent dancing,
holding a sax in my arms,
swaying in the hazy drunkenness
of people who don't give a rat's ass
about anything but the groove.

I can listen to the rain,
watch it drip off the brim of my fedora
as I lie myself back into a younger body,
into bodies that never touched
but in thought.

And it is for these lies
I give thanks,
carve my life into small pieces
like notes on a register,
and blow through a moist reed.

My fingers
move over the keys
as though I were loosening a zipper,
unhooking a bra,
feeling her skin wrap around me
like a bandage to heal
all that got broken in the fields.

But she is like a porch swing
with a frayed rope,
the weight of the wind
is almost too much.

A bird song
just might be enough
to bring the whole house crashing down.

Walking Stones

i was born in the spring in 1958 in a country clearly my own

i was born embracing my father's drawl
his curly hair
the agate of his eye
before my own eyes had barely opened

my mother's suffering erected an orphanage around me
this mirror of her own childhood filled with farm chores
pickup trucks beans in the pressure cooker
exhaling steam on the windows

i barely noticed the F-104 Starfighter
breaking the world speed record
as the Sunday steeples trembled above the town
and the statue of the doughboy
looked down from the steps of city hall
over the lives of those he died for

all i saw was the light that surrounded me
like ten suns that raised me up in its arms
gave me a name that burned
Bible verses onto my tongue and erected a Berlin Wall
within my soul to keep out
the Castros and their firing squads

i was born to fill the quiet
with the silence of the graveyard
all those stories of the past whispering
through the new shoots of grass
and unfurling in the tips of leaves
waiting to be retold and not forgotten

i was made to be that constant fire
in the bed of a nappy headed girl
as our lives entwine into a great vine
branching out in all directions
and we speak this language of coal
in low underground flames

i was born with the Blue Ridge Mountains
running the length of my spine
with its forests of flowering dogwoods

sugar maple hemlocks and white oak

i emerged just as the spirit of Jacob Fichman
ascended into the heavens
and left a little residue of the holy ghost on my forehead

i came from nothing
and had nothing but dream to sustain me

i was born to be like one of those stones in the desert
that moves a fraction of an inch each day
in spite of gravity
that leaves a trail through the dirt for others to follow
and they do

Bedtime Stories

The book opens with a soft swoosh of owl wings.
Archimedes settles onto his perch.
Mother's voice carries the boy resting
on his pillow to the hills surrounding Camelot
where horses' hooves clomp over cobblestones,
armor and swords rattle, and knights chatter
heading through the city square where one day
they'll take their seat of wisdom at the round table.
He hears a faint metallic ring as the sword slides from stone
and the crowd of onlookers gasps in unison at such a waif.
Her tone grows shrill as Uther and Morgana hatch
their plots for power, and Merlin, in love and out of love,
returns to rescue his beloved Arthur and Excalibur.
The boy fidgets when she talks harshly of the cuckolded king,
the clandestine lovers, their dark secret
that could destroy the kingdom. Then when his tired
eyes finally close, she shuts the book, pulls the spread
over his shoulders, the same ritual each night.
In the hushed room, she peers into a face
innocent as dew, feels the gentle wing-beats
of his soul searching out the holy grail of words.

Film Noir

call me anything you want

call me the savior of moonshine
unfit to lick your Daddy's boots

call me those myths of regret reborn
that lie even when they are telling the truth

tell me
I'm the wound that opens like Salvidor Dali's eye
in the dark night of your soul

call me the allegory of a burnt tick
jerking through your dreams
in 16mm

in mine
words scale your body
like liana
for all the junkies to climb

call me sphinx
built by the slaves of love
the riddle you can never solve

on the hottest nights
I always leave the screen door unlatched
let the whirling of the fan
whisper your name
across the fields

call me singed hair
clinging to the bullet of a song
before you slap me

you're the lipstick print
left on the empty bottle by my nightstand

that alibi
for all my futures
forking perpetually through time

tell me which one to take

Seeding the World with Psalms and Parables

I asked God if it was okay to be melodramatic
and he said you dummy do whatever you want

he wasn't a puppet master pulling everyone's strings
he wanted more credit than that and said
don't think of him as Zeus enthroned on Olympus
getting his rocks off playing jokes on the mortals below
or Yahweh handing down the law from a burning bush
atop a desert mountain or Allah sonless and fatherless
alone in the heavens seeing every deed hearing every thought

he kicked me in the shin and said cry to your heart's content
wring out a dishrag of tears scream at the sky or the ground
take my name in vain write your poems and novels
about the injustice of it all sing your songs
say your prayers twist your words into idols others may worship
your agony is real and your existence is meaningless as intended

when the visit was over the orderly wheeled him
back into the nursing home a smile blooming
into a field of clover on the old trickster's face
and as he disappeared he waved
the back of his hand toward me

saying now go forth and create my son
be your own little god
go build your own universe
and see if you can do better

Neighbors

a boy is born into a great country
twenty years pass
now he is just a dead soldier
almost unrecognizable in desert sands
the same boy who came to our rescue
carrying a basket of peaches up the stairs
and two or three fell out
tumbled down the steps
the sound mingling
with the everyday sounds of the world
and we watched him pause for a moment
to listen to the songs
coming from a stone birdbath
the different pitch in each voice

Why Can't Every Man Be Like Moses?

1.

Grasshoppers descend upon the fields
disguised as God's wrath. Even the philosophers
are baffled. Seven fat years give way
to seven lean years. Now Pharaoh
tastes the bitterness of the people's poverty,
feels his teeth crack on the hard truths
left untouched by the rats
in the royal grain cellars.

2.

Poverty is the whetstone of philosophers
and poets. One moment you think
you're a king building pyramids of stone
cut and shaped from the sky's quarries;
the next moment you embrace
your blood lineage, wander for forty years
in the wilderness searching for a Promised Land
that exists just beyond you fingertips
as the journey grinds you down to dust in the fields
and the grasshoppers sing their ancient song
over the bodies of thousands like you.

3.

What is poverty but a different kind
of richness? Grasshoppers leap
from one blade of grass to another.
They know nothing of a river turning red,
a mist descending to take the first born males,
or the sea opening to let one people slip through
while swallowing the pursuing army. Philosophers
whisper in the leaves above your head. The Law
is handed down as wind and rain carve
rock into a serene majesty. There in the sun-baked fields
where sheep and goats gnaw tufts of Johnson grass
and the thistles' purple flowers
your bride awaits in dirty jeans, smiling as you approach.

La Dolce Vita

I'm living deeply now
like the earthworm, that patient farmer
who tills the soil into bloom.

Yet who really respects him? And does he care?

Roots leak through the roof of his house,
his floor is cobbled with stone
and he speaks in mouthfuls of dirt.

All his waking hours are spent
in the workshop carving doorways,
channels that lead through his kingdom of loam.

No north star guides his eternal nights.
He navigates on feel alone.

But he's always there when I spade open
the garden in spring, pink as a cherry blossom,
kissing the ground like some old Italian winemaker
still anxious to savor all life has to offer.

Scrooged

Old Marley, dead as a doornail, and no words
can bring him back. The counting house continues to churn
out money like a candle whose flame can't be extinguished,
but it warms no one, not even the open palm
held just above its yellow swath of light.
So much is darkness now, dear nephew,
that I long for the return of the ghosts
to harden my spirit back into black obsidian.
Everywhere I go in the city the hands
of ragamuffins reach out for a coin, a scrap
of bread, a pat on the head, millions of them.
This city is nothing but a bottomless well
and I'm falling, always falling, waiting for the thud
of bottom. It's like looking into your mother's eyes,
into Belle's eyes, the black drawing me in deeper
and deeper until I know longer know who I am.
What happened to Scrooge, everyone asks,
has he completely gone mad? Little do they know
I have. There's else nothing left to give, so I place my hand
on the robe of the third ghost to lead me
through the rusted iron gates toward that final resting place
where once again I can warm my crooked fingers
over the small coal-fire of my soul knowing
Cratchit is still hard at work on the other side of the door.

Walt Whitman Service Area, NJTP

As the needle inches toward E
I spot the sign, 5 miles to go.
Fumes or not, I have an appointment
to keep. Not with the gas station
attendant, whose union won't let anyone
pump their own gas, or the TCBY
workers whose frozen yogurts
taste as sweet as the real
thing or the Burger King flunkies
scenting the parking lot with their charbroiled
offerings. The turnpike exit fades into
scarred pavement, the mini-mall's façade
is torn down, steel 2x4s nailed into position
for a face lift. I ease to a stop between
the emptiness of dirt white lines.
The sweltering heat embraces me with
its afternoon shimmer as my
eyes scan the horizon. Then I see
him, there behind the buildings, the good
grey heron striding through a ditch of black
water. His eyes are blue as the bards
of Camden. They stare me down, baptize
my image in the mirrors of their lakes.
                                        "Walt,"
I want to say, "today your books may rot
in the used stalls and school kids laugh
at your bravado, but I've come here to find
you again, reincarnated, a plume
of feathers atop your head. My words
have become nothing more than the cardboard
butterflies you used to balance on your fingertips
as you posed before the photographers.
A bit of old-age trickery. I need you to teach me
the joy of myself, how to balance my soul
on a blade of grass, catch a ray
of sunlight with my tongue." He croaks
his understanding as he swallows
something bitter that could be my heart,
unfurls his wings to fly into a lone pine tree.
My song of the open road continues
with the rush of tires on pavement,

the wind parting my hair, and a feather
taped to the rear view mirror
to remind me where I am going.

as I slice open

the package
I received in the mail
from the used bookstore

the smell of evergreens
overwhelms me
fir trees
from the black forest

snow falling
through the stiff needles
then I open
the yellowed pages

read the first few words
and *kristallnacht*
descends over me
in a shower of stars

the shoah train
pulls away
from the station in a puff
of steam and ashes

wolves
in their grey uniforms
scavenge fields and villages
howl out on the steppes

as the worst dreams
of Hansel and Gretel
finally
come true

Soliloquy of the Interior Paramour

For years I knew only nights, blackness,
the blind words of damp streets.

I followed their unraveling to narrow rooms
where the sleepless talked to no one.

I crouched in doorways hidden by golden clouds of tobacco
as zippers slid and cash slapped hands.

I heard the piston of the heart creak
its uneven *I want, I want,* lurch toward

some kind of unloneliness, where the landscape
is momentarily peopled by need.

Not once did it call out my name, even
as the mind painted me into existence.

Afterwards, on walks down to the docks,
past the bar lights, the all night Laundromats,

I danced to the string music of his soul.
Waltzes, nothing but waltzes. ¾ time, swirling

like the eddies of the river, collecting
the flotsam of lives I couldn't even see.

But he who bore me was empty, empty,
a maelstrom that pulled me under to give me voice.

Portrait with Water

The clock in her chest has no hands.
To tell time she drags a razor across skin.
Blood freckles her leg. A trickle of seconds.
Death by the hundred thousands.
Death in each scrape of shaving cream washed down the drain.
Each breath that fogs the mirror.
Exhausted, she rises to the tap of rain on the window.
Branches scratch the wall with their shadows.
Fingers of charcoal that animate the semi-darkness.
Johnnie Walker on the rocks. Coltrane on the stereo.
Her nightgown slides to the floor.
Smooth as honey without the sting.
The wolf-growl of thunder, eye-flash of lightning.
The dog's howl and tremble.
Bathwater warm as a new layer of skin.
Raindrops heavy as pebbles on the skylight.
Those lessons elemental as the passing of seasons.
Difficult as the calculus of the heart.
The swirling notes of the sax can't help her.
The liquor. The hiss of tires rushing through streets.
She sinks lethargically into lilac-scented bubbles.
The anonymous faces ghosting before the window.
Another thing she can't see coming.

Farewell

When I am dead, my dearest,
uncurl the pencil from my fingers,
leave the smudge of writing on my cheek.

These last lines are my tattoo of love
for you and this life, both of which
I did not cherish as much as deserved.

Bury me with this beauty mark
on my face, the undying symbol
of my devotion to you and my art.

But keep my memory and my poems
pressed like a rose between the pages
of your heart, even when another

comes into your life (like I know
he will), takes over my side of the bed,
curls around you comfortably as a spoon.

www.ingramcontent.com/pod-product-compliance
Lightning Source LLC
LaVergne TN
LVHW011405080426
835511LV00005B/412